A Royal Invitation

Roz Innes

A ROYAL INVITATION

Artwork by Dominique Driver (Instagram: dominique.driver) and Erin Innes

Author Photo by Moya Photography - http://www.moyaphotography.nz/

Editing by Anna's Editing, New Zealand. – facebook.com/Annas.Editing.Co

Prepared for publishing by Wordwyze Publishing Ltd, New Zealand
http://wordwyze.nz

A catalogue record for this book is available from the
National Library of New Zealand.
Copies of this book are available direct from the author by emailing
rozinnes.creative@gmail.com
or can be ordered from any bookstore or library worldwide.

ISBN: 978-0-473-62255-8

Dedications

This anthology of devotions is dedicated first and foremost to wonderful Father God, Jesus, and the Holy Spirit, whose keeping power always amazes me. He uses ordinary people to perpetuate His will and ways. This project has shown this to be true.

To my wonderful husband, Roy, my greatest cheerleader. He has always encouraged me in the things of God and has been true to what he said on our wedding day thirty-three years ago: "If God tells you to do anything, do it, as long as you don't break anything because I'll have to pay for it."

To Erin, Tegan, Jared and future grand-children and family.

To those who hunger and thirst for His kingdom to come on earth as it is in heaven.

Foreword

Roz shares with us the authentic whispers in the heart of humanity as we respond to the glorious truth embedded within Scripture. In this daily devotional, you will be drawn into the manifestation of Scriptural truth that will transform your inner world. I have known Roz for many years and have witnessed her steadfast walk with God through the highs and lows that life inevitably brings. This text is a testament of her journey through the fire that has uncovered gold. Those that walk with this devotional will discover more of the nature of God and experience the transforming work of the Spirit.

Lynley Allan
Senior Leader, Catch the Fire, Auckland

I have known Roz as a personal friend for many years and was delighted to be asked to write this foreword.

With her passion for sharing her faith with the world, I know that Roz has poured her heart and soul into this little devotional book. I hope that many people will gain from her wisdom, as I have done over the years.

Pat Backley
Author of Daisy and The Second Daisy

Invincible you

Indelibly invested in all you do

A creation and not a mistake.

He's come to strip away all

and everything fake.

It's not works or education or gain

But a choice to trust Him –

the only thing that will remain.

R. Innes

Preface

Dear Reader,

Welcome to my 40-day devotional.

Like most of you, I have been faced with numerous tests and trials since committing my life to God. His Word and presence have strengthened me and enabled me to persevere. This is my prayer for you.

I have been challenged to use scripture more actively in situations and to experience the dynamic power of a change of perspective. My heart's desire is to see more people standing strong in their faith despite the stresses of life.

The insights of the 40 chosen scriptures are not exhaustive and serve rather as a launching pad for what God is saying to you in your walk with Him.

His Word is changing us.

Blessing you as you accept your royal invitation.

> *Those who sow their tears as seeds will reap a harvest with joyful shouts of glee. (Psalm 126:5 TPT)*

Lord, thank You that the times we've come to You troubled and harassed, You have not been put off by our weakness. Rather, You have drawn us near with whispers of love and hope. Our brokenness has been pieced together, bit by bit, with shepherd's hands. Like a watchman we wait, anticipating the harvest ready for its season.

You teach us the joy in trusting!

Prayer: Your kingdom come, Your will be done... in faith and patience I receive your promises, the harvest of my prayers. Your timing and Your way, Lord.

God is saying to me:

_____

_____

_____

_____

_____

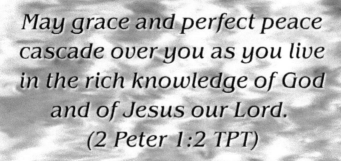

May grace and perfect peace cascade over you as you live in the rich knowledge of God and of Jesus our Lord.
(2 Peter 1:2 TPT)

Echoing the Spirit, the natural world. Repeated beautiful rhythms and cycles magnify Your faithfulness – day and night, summer, winter, autumn and spring. In Your perfect abiding, Your grace and peace come. We are enlarged in the knowing of You, with more grace and peace. More grace and peace with more knowing of You.

Liquid love pouring – You embrace us today!

Prayer: Your powerful abiding presence is my rock and fortress today and every day, and Your love is my provision in all circumstances.

God is saying to me:

_____

_____

_____

_____

_____

> God spoke: "Light!" And light appeared.
> God saw that light was good and
> separated light from dark. God named the
> light Day, he named the dark Night. It was
> evening, it was morning - Day One.
> (Genesis 1:3-5 MSG)

The birth of a baby; a couple starting out their married life together; the start of a new season – what a joy new beginnings are. Completed moments of time and creation, giving rise to the commencement of different cycles. The first day of creation started in the evening, in the stillness of time with nothing to see but darkness. Our seasons give rise to fruitfulness and new beginnings even when hidden with lack of clarity from our natural eyes.

It will be good!

Prayer: You separate darkness and lies from light and truth – I choose to believe and trust Your ways of creating pleasing results in my life. You deliver me from the situation or provide for me through it – growing me spiritually either way.

God is saying to me:

_____

_____

_____

_____

> *Paul, an apostle of Christ Jesus*
> *through the will of God...*
> *(Ephesians 1:1 WEB)*

When we are born, our parents usually choose our names according to family tradition, in memory of a friend, or perhaps because they like the meaning or sound of the name. Did you know that God knows your name? Not only that, but He knew everything about you before you were born, and it filled Him with delight. He also calls you holy, beloved, chosen, forgiven, and his son or daughter.

Our hearts are full as we take hold of Your intimate knowledge of us and Your amazing grace.

Prayer: Creator and life-giver, each of us reflects You. I choose to mirror You today – Your goodness, Your grace and Your love. Our hearts are full as we take hold of Your intimate knowledge of us and Your amazing grace.

God is saying to me:

_____

_____

_____

_____

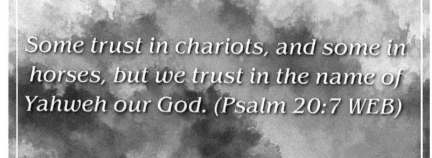

Some trust in chariots, and some in horses, but we trust in the name of Yahweh our God. (Psalm 20:7 WEB)

Victorious and conquering. Peace-leading, love-drawing, the provision is available for us, with answers coming in unexpected packages – there for the taking. Trusting in Your finished work.

Faithful God – consistent in covenant – Your Word is truth.

Prayer: There is no one to compare with You, my hero and champion. Everything that happens to me will have good, eternal outcomes because of Your plans for me.

God is saying to me:

_____

_____

_____

_____

_____

_____

> *I want a walk in the country,*
> *I want a cabin in the woods.*
> *I'm desperate for a change from*
> *rage and stormy weather.*
> *(Psalm 55:8 MSG)*

What reassurance and comfort we have knowing that You, Jesus, are in every situation with us, through the storms and trials of life. When circumstances appear to be too difficult to handle, even then You are near. You are there – and as the master of the universe You are not affected or overcome by anything. We are your chosen, beloved children. We rest confidently in your promises and look for your upgrade of provision.

Prayer: I know everything works for my benefit – I trust Your provisions and outcomes. I am in training to reign with You and will choose to see Your perspectives in what I experience.

God is saying to me:

_____

_____

_____

_____

_____

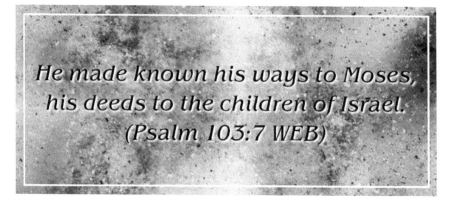

He made known his ways to Moses, his deeds to the children of Israel. (Psalm 103:7 WEB)

Challenging us to be close... deep calls to deep. Abba (Daddy), we desire You more than anything else. Teach us Your ways and instruct us in how to please You.

The loving comes first, the needs after. Master of all, we delight in trusting You, knowing You delight in us.

Prayer: I intentionally choose Your ways. I hunger and thirst for intimacy and the deeds of righteousness that are the result of knowing You. Be Lord of all I am today.

God is saying to me:

_____

_____

_____

_____

_____

_____

> *Simon and those who were with him searched for him. They found him and told him, "Everyone is looking for you." (Mark 1:36-37 WEB)*

Purposefully and intentionally, we search for You. Not a glance of no cost, but a seeking. Closer, closer, You are coaxing us, nearer and deeper – receiving Your living Spirit water now. Cuddling up nearer. My need is more of You, Lord. We respond in harmony with You, resting, receiving perfect times. *Selah.*

Prayer: Only You satisfy and fill me with Yourself... there is nothing and no one to compare with You. You reward me with Your beautiful presence as I seek You in private places within.

God is saying to me:

_____

_____

_____

_____

_____

_____

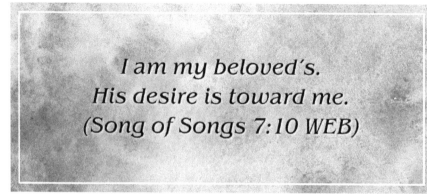

I am my beloved's.
His desire is toward me.
(Song of Songs 7:10 WEB)

Calling, beckoning, yearning, gently He calls us to come higher. His essence of greatness and kindness – awareness now, swirling into waves of refreshing and embrace. A filling and resting, a resting and filling. Closer and closer until lines between us are blurred into oneness. Moving to higher places, being immersed in Him.

Prayer: Today I choose the carefree stance of being Your adored one, the one Your heart is committed to. Use all of me today and give me more understanding of who You are.

God is saying to me:

_____

_____

_____

_____

_____

_____

> *...what mighty miracles and your power at work, just to name a few. Depths of purpose and layers of meaning saturate everything you do. (Psalm 92:5 TPT)*

Nuances and shades of the essence of You all around. From whispers of love and contended smiles to ecstatic embrace and bursts of outpouring joy. Come beloved, draw near, He calls to us. He pours himself gladly into us with gifts of grace and love and tenderness.

Prayer: I know Your plans for me go way beyond anything I could imagine – today I surrender myself to be used to draw others to You. Give me Your insight and passion for the plans You have for those around me.

God is saying to me:

_____

_____

_____

_____

_____

> *Be still, and know that I am God.*
> *I will be exalted among the nations.*
> *I will be exalted in the earth.*
> *(Psalm 46:10 WEB)*

I am what you need in every situation today. I will be the answer and the One who you desire me to be. Come and rest with Me and I will show you the best way... the way of quiet and confidence bears testimony of my control. I will do what is best for you – my beloved!

Prayer: Mighty creator of the beginning and end of all things, I worship You for who You are. Things in my life that need an end I commit to You. I trust for a fresh new season of Your purposes for me.

God is saying to me:

_____

_____

_____

_____

_____

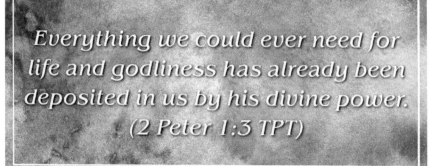

Everything we could ever need for life and godliness has already been deposited in us by his divine power. (2 Peter 1:3 TPT)

My love, we will adventure in the Spirit now, to a new place of overcoming, where I am near – your guide and champion. My faithfulness will show that my promises are true. My provision is there, let's find a treasure for you! Joy, hope, peace and love, my Word is showing you – trust Me. I give you power to live above every harassment because you are mine.

Prayer: Rest and hope for every situation is my inheritance today, Lord. You are greater than every worry and concern. I hear You whisper, "You can do it!" and know You are confident in my ability to overcome.

God is saying to me:

_____

_____

_____

_____

_____

If your spirit burns with light, fully illuminated with no trace of darkness, you will be a shining lamp, reflecting rays of truth by the way you live.
(Luke 11:36 TPT)

Lord, today we choose to upgrade our thinking and live in the truth of being loved by You and loving others. We choose to outwork actions of love, joy and peace, that make us a lamp, shining, for others to follow. Representing You is an honour; we reflect Your light in our lives. You are the mirror we see ourselves and others in.

Prayer: You are the epitome of life bursting at the seams – the kernel of abundant life of Father, Son and Spirit. You live in me. I will shine for You today!

God is saying to me:

_____

_____

_____

_____

_____

> *The place where your treasure is, is the place you will most want to be, and end up being.*
> *(Luke 12:34 MSG)*

Jesus is urging us to intentionally and deliberately have a mindset of seeking and investing in things pertaining to God's kingdom. He will guard all that we invest in time, money, effort and sacrifice, and it will be given back with interest. As we start doing this, our attention and love for His kingdom increases – what an amazing spinoff!

Prayer: Lord, I remember that the things that are truly precious are the things You say are valuable – hope, faith and love. I am Your child and today I choose to use these precepts as my faithful guide.

God is saying to me:

_____

_____

_____

_____

_____

> *Can you not discern this new day*
> *of destiny breaking forth around you?*
> *The early signs of my purposes*
> *and plans are bursting forth.*
> *(Song of Songs 2:13a TPT)*

Master of the increase, today we come to You. You have planned every season of our lives to reflect provision and hope. You are near and bring eternal purpose to everything, pain and pleasure, grief and joy. How sweet it is to trust You – faithful, loving and omniscient.

Prayer: You are always wanting to do something with me, around me and inside me. I want to be enlarged in knowing Your love for me. I believe Your plans will always cause goodness and mercy to show themselves in my life.

God is saying to me:

_____

_____

_____

_____

_____

Your spiritual roots go deeply into his life as you are continually infused with strength, encouraged in every way. For you are established in the faith you have absorbed and enriched by your devotion to him! (Col 2:7 TPT)

Our lives are becoming firmly established in His truths and we are becoming increasingly like Him. Just like a seed grows to genetically reproduce all that is in its DNA, we are being called into all that is pure, lovely and truthful. Our thought patterns renewed, we are established as fruit-bearing plants for You, wonderful lover of our souls!

Prayer: I receive an infusion of Your wholeness and encouragement for every circumstance that is bothering me. You have experienced and understand every uncomfortable and painful situation. What joy there is in knowing that You give me victory over everything trying to defeat me.

God is saying to me:

_____

_____

_____

_____

_____

> *So let God work His will in you.*
> *Yell a loud NO to the devil*
> *and watch him scamper.*
> *Say a quiet YES to God*
> *and He'll be there in no time.*
> *(James 4:7 MSG)*

Heart turning, recognition dawning, love's language speaking. New times of seeing and knowing You today, Father God. We believe Your promise, that surrender to You guarantees a withdrawal of the devil's plans. Victory won, Your Word and presence – a banner of love over us. Lead us to Your banqueting table of life.

Prayer: Today I choose to walk in the obedience of Your plans for me. I will have new mindsets and believe that Your ways of thinking are best. Child-like wonder of You will regulate my responses to You and others.

God is saying to me:

_____

_____

_____

_____

_____

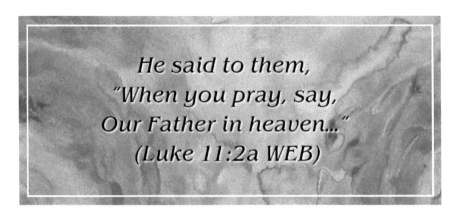

He said to them,
"When you pray, say,
Our Father in heaven..."
(Luke 11:2a WEB)

Today we acknowledge You, God, as our Daddy, Papa, Abba – the One who loves us more than any earthly father. Not only do You love, but You are love. Your capacity and heart towards us always lead us to greater perspectives in every circumstance. You draw us close and show us Your bigger plan so that we cannot help but respond to You.

Prayer: Every part of my life reflects your love and care. You are a wonderful companion, faithful friend, and perfect father. Today I remember Your provision in difficult times and trust You with everything about the present and future.

God is saying to me:

_____

_____

_____

_____

_____

> *But I will sacrifice to you*
> *with the voice of thanksgiving.*
> *(Jonah 2:9a WEB)*

Smiling and drawing close with irresistible longing, You find me in my prayers and songs of gratitude. God of the universe, who names the stars and breathes life into every creature, You delight in my delighting of You.

Prayer: My thanks and praise go beyond loving You for what You give. My sacrifice of worship is because You are worthy even when times and seasons don't seem to be working out. God of justice, grace and peace – the originator of everything that is beautiful – I celebrate You loving me!

God is saying to me:

_____

_____

_____

_____

_____

_____

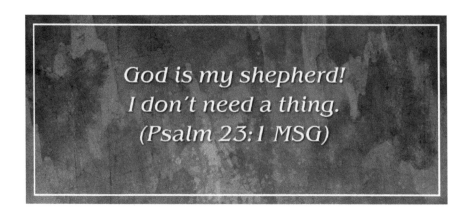

*God is my shepherd!
I don't need a thing.
(Psalm 23:1 MSG)*

We are the sheep of the Shepherd – He gives us rest and leads us to the oasis of peace and restores and revives us. He teaches us through His nearness how to be strong and brave. We are given a place of honour at His table of provision as we enjoy Him today.

Prayer: You care for me today and every day. Your eyes watch me and You work out every detail of my life to please You. I partner with Your plans and accept Your provision.

God is saying to me:

_____

_____

_____

_____

_____

_____

> *Standing behind at his feet weeping,*
> *she began to wet his feet with her tears,*
> *and she wiped them with the hair*
> *of her head, kissed his feet,*
> *and anointed them with the ointment.*
> *(Luke 7:38 WEB)*

A beautiful memorial to an amazing God.

Karov in Hebrew means "to come near". We come near to You, Lord, and we offer our thoughts and behaviours as worthy sacrifices to You, beloved King. May You further your will and intentions as we choose to align ourselves to Your heart and ways.

Prayer: My offering of bringing heaven to earth through words and actions will touch Your heart too, Lord. I choose to let my tears and kisses be used for Your purposes.

God is saying to me:

_____

_____

_____

_____

_____

_____

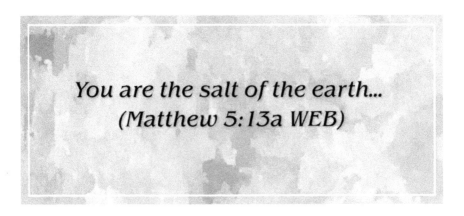

You are the salt of the earth...
(Matthew 5:13a WEB)

We are saturated and salted by Your Spirit, overflowing with praise – Lord, we will enjoy these intimate moments with You. We remember and reflect on Your goodness. Enfolded in Your love and kissed by Your grace we crave for more abundant life in You.

Prayer: May the reality of Your love in me result in making people want to know You. Lead me, through Your Spirit, to quench the thirst of those who have tasted the salt of Your Word. Give me courage to share Your heart with others.

God is saying to me:

_____

_____

_____

_____

_____

_____

> *...I passionately love your revelation-light!*
> *You're my place of quiet retreat, and your*
> *wrap-around presence becomes my shield*
> *as I wrap myself in your word!*
> *(Psalm 119:113-114 TPT)*

Jesus is the Word of God, and the Word of God is Him. A shelter, a protection, a defence, and a truth imparter. Vision giver and wonderful helper – our lover, wooing and whispering plans and promises.

Prayer: You are my revelation-giver today, the one who gives me a part in your eternal love and purposes. Beautiful redeemer – showing me past, present and future facets of eternity that work together for your glory. Worthy of trust, You are a covenant God.

God is saying to me:

_____

_____

_____

_____

_____

_____

> *Let each one test His own actions*
> *so that He can be proud of himself*
> *alone, without comparing himself*
> *with someone else.*
> *(Galatians 6:4 TPT)*

Today we celebrate Your amazing grace. We are co-heirs and joint rulers with You in heavenly places. Your gift of life and grace in us has enabled us to choose a life rich in works, motivated by love, joy and peace. Built on these marvellous foundations, we dedicate our words and actions to You. This is our memorial of love to You, beautiful king and saviour.

Prayer: Preparing, encouraging, and guiding; You are showing me where to go and what to do. May my thoughts and actions today align with what You mean to me. I choose your paths of love, hope and faith, and offer them back to You. *Selah.*

God is saying to me:

_____

_____

_____

_____

_____

> *...when your faith is tested, it stirs up power within you to endure all things. And then as your endurance grows even stronger it will release perfection into every part of your being until there is nothing missing and nothing lacking. (James 1:3 TPT)*

The sublime echo of wholeness and completeness beckons as we lean upon You today. We partake of your goodness and trust it to be more than enough for what we are experiencing. We receive by faith, Your sufficiency today.

You in us and us in You – more than enough!

Prayer: With courage, I take another step towards You on the highway of wholeness; You are the essence of all that I need. Seeking You before anything else, You will bring me everything I need when I need it.

God is saying to me:

_____

_____

_____

_____

_____

> *...we absorb God's Word, which has been implanted within our nature, for the Word of Life has power to continually deliver us.*
> *(James 1:21b TPT)*

Jesus, You are the Word made flesh and Your beautiful Spirit calls to us to embrace Your overflowing, overcoming life. We rise with You to realms of possibility and hope in every circumstance and choose Your carefree attitude of rest and trust.

Prayer: I commit my thoughts and actions to You. Today, I trust Your ability to use me. My obedience will be a part of Your magnificent plan for the people around me.

God is saying to me:

_____

_____

_____

_____

_____

_____

> *He alone is my rock*
> *and my salvation, my fortress.*
> *I will not be shaken.*
> *(Psalm 62:6 WEB)*

Near You, snuggled next to Your heart, is our safe space. We find that place each of us uniquely fills in Your heart. Boundaries of fear and doubt blur and Your love seeps into every space of our beings. We partner with You, beloved Saviour, as deep calls to deep and where nothing separates us.

There is nothing else needed. Selah.

Prayer: My needs are fulfilled because of who You are; the great "I Am". Whatever I need You to be today You will be, because of Your amazing love.

God is saying to me:

_____

_____

_____

_____

_____

> *God, you are my God.*
> *I will earnestly seek you.*
> *My soul thirsts for you.*
> *My flesh longs for you, in a dry*
> *and weary land, where there is no water.*
> *(Psalm 63:1 WEB)*

Focusing on You, we determine to find Your presence within. Like a dry sponge we soak up Your provision and experience your kindness and grace. Always there, You are who we long to be with and the one we desire to reflect – irresistible God!

Prayer: You give meaning and purpose to living. Everything in your kingdom co-ordinates itself in perfect rhythm and harmony. Today let me be part of bringing that into my world.

God is saying to me:

_____

_____

_____

_____

_____

_____

> *I continue to pray for your love to grow*
> *and increase beyond measure,*
> *bringing you into the rich revelation*
> *of spiritual insight in all things.*
> *(Phil 1:9 TPT)*

Love is the currency of His kingdom. The upside-down kingdom of giving then receiving, humility leading to promotion, and faith leading to impossibilities. Dare to believe Him today for the unimaginable – that circumstance that needs a miracle.

He is willing and able!

Prayer: Today may I be part of your magnificent plan of being loved and giving that love away. You are teaching me more about your ways and how to return to that state of perfect fellowship and love towards You, myself and others.

God is saying to me:

_____

_____

_____

_____

_____

> *For by him all things were created,*
> *in the heavens and on the earth,*
> *things visible and things invisible,*
> *whether thrones or dominions or principalities*
> *or powers; all things have been created*
> *through him, and for him. (Col. 1:16 WEB)*

You were... You are and always will be. Eternal, omnipotent and omniscient – our wonderful Father. Through You, triune God, all things were initiated and made. Speak Your Word and universes appear. You are the fabric of all substance, and we are one with You through Jesus' amazing sacrifice.

Prayer: I was created because of You and for Your pleasure. That propels and galvanises my heart to respond to You with sacrifices shaped by love.

God is saying to me:

_____

_____

_____

_____

_____

> *...Jesus spoke to them, saying,*
> *"I am the light of the world.*
> *He who follows me will not walk*
> *in the darkness, but will have*
> *the light of life". (John 8:12 WEB)*

Looking intently through rainbow spectrums of the light of emotions and perspectives of this world, we find Your illuminating presence – pure and definitive. You are the essence of creation, illuminating brightness, all-consuming lover of our souls.

Prayer: Signposting my life path, You illuminate the most excellent responses for me to walk in today – thank You, Lord! You are always calling me into Your ways of wisdom and light.

God is saying to me:

_____

_____

_____

_____

_____

_____

_____

> *Take advantage of every opportunity to be a blessing to others.*
> *(Galatians 6:10 TPT)*

We choose to allow Your measure of goodness in us to change circumstances and situations today. Your grace in us actions us to give. We will use the words of our mouths and the deeds of our hands to give hope, comfort and life.

Prayer: I want to see You in others and to choose to spread Your love according to the measure of grace You have given me. Give me discernment to know when a need in others is overwhelming, and to know when I am the answer to that.

God is saying to me:

_____

_____

_____

_____

_____

_____

> *I will answer your cry for help*
> *every time you pray,*
> *and you will find and feel my presence*
> *even in your time of pressure and trouble.*
> *I will be your glorious hero*
> *and give you a feast. (Psalm 91:15 TPT)*

Always patient, ever-present God, near to us. Your hope and love hover on the edge of consciousness, always ready to save and deliver. You are the knight in shining armour who comes to give victory to us, your beloved ones – loosening strangleholds of circumstance.

We see and experience Your deliverance.

Prayer: Father, You have said that those poor in spirit are blessed and to be envied. Your kingdom belongs to this group of child-like people who are not self-reliant. I come to You with expectation – one who needs You today!

God is saying to me:

_____

_____

_____

_____

_____

> *...every word he speaks is full of revelation and becomes a fountain of understanding within you. For the Lord has a hidden storehouse of wisdom, made accessible to his godly lovers. (Proverbs 2:6 TPT)*

Holy Spirit, Your amazing God-perspectives lead us. We follow Your revealed light and choose Your ways. Your love is a very present help with everything we will encounter today.

Word of God and Spirit of God, our victory is in You!

Prayer: The ways of understanding and wisdom are the choice of my heart today, Lord. I receive in faith more of Your gifts of love, joy, peace, kindness and goodness towards You, myself and others.

God is saying to me:

_____

_____

_____

_____

_____

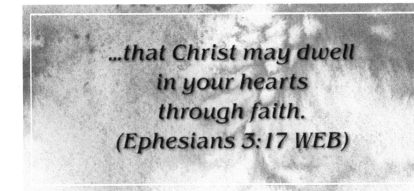

...that Christ may dwell in your hearts through faith. (Ephesians 3:17 WEB)

Not just a visit, but God with us. Eternity in our hearts – depths of love and faith that will never end. Your permanence is so reassuring – You give us all we need through the layers of yourself that keep and comfort. Your perspectives reign through lives committed to following Love's footsteps.

Prayer: Show me what it means to have Your Spirit living in my heart. I honour You as the Lord of my choices today as I engage with this world that You died for. I receive the gifts of grace You have for me and those around me.

God is saying to me:

_____

_____

_____

_____

_____

> *One who is slow to anger is better than the mighty; one who rules his spirit, than he who takes a city.*
> *(Proverbs 16:32 WEB)*

Intentionally, we clothe our minds with your shalom peace, running to that place in You where nothing is missing and nothing is broken. We choose to live in your provision, decisively taking control over ourselves. Living to represent the one who is master of every situation.

Prayer: Many envy warriors their strength, but I want to have the self-control of the merciful. I will my filter responses through the lens of your Word.

God is saying to me:

_____

_____

_____

_____

_____

_____

> *For we have the living Word of God,*
> *which is full of energy,*
> *like a two-mouthed sword.*
> *(Hebrews 4:12 TPT)*

Bringing change, reinforcing, defining and defending all He represents – the Living Word. The Holy Spirit ignites the written words of life. We bask in the revelation of being loved by the Father, in the same way that He loves Jesus. Two mouths of testimony in living words, bearing witness of truth.

Prayer: Speak and call us to deep waters of intimacy and grace. Reveal Yourself to us face to face. *Selah.*

God is saying to me:

_____

_____

_____

_____

_____

_____

_____

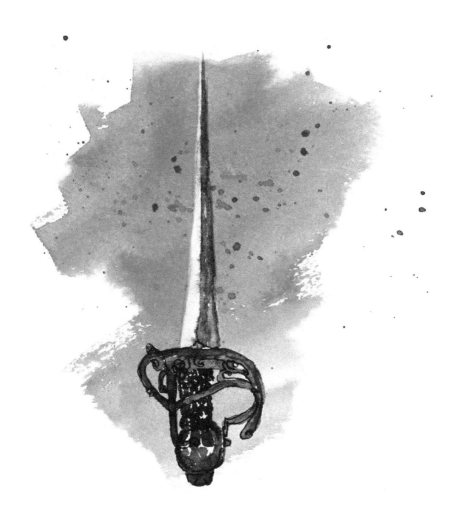

> *He's been through weakness and testing, experienced it all – all but the sin.*
> *(Hebrews 4:15 MSG)*

What a joy to know You understand everything about us! Joy, heartache, trial and testing... You are master of the full spectrum of experiences and circumstances. We comfort ourselves in You, beloved high priest of our salvation. We believe You are bringing us to an upgraded renewal in You.

Prayer: I trust Your outcomes and Your answers. Answers through Your Word, to deliver me from situations, or that You will be more than enough in them. I take hold of those eternal benefits.

God is saying to me:

_____

_____

_____

_____

_____

_____

> *So above all else,*
> *let love be the beautiful prize*
> *for which you run.*
> *(1 Corinthians 13:13b TPT)*

The ultimate prize, His kingdom's glory. Love is His relational plan. A perfect mandate of a fantastic God. There are many ways to bridge the divide between His love and fallen earth. A transference of encounter to transformation and overflow.

Prayer: Work Your kingdom plan, Lord, and massage truth into my heart. Open my eyes and show me how to intentionally love You and others today.

God is saying to me:

_____

_____

_____

_____

_____

_____

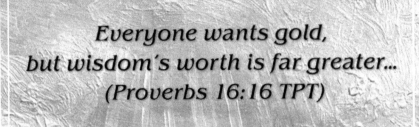

*Everyone wants gold,
but wisdom's worth is far greater...
(Proverbs 16:16 TPT)*

The upside-down kingdom of God is where currency of value is shockingly different. Wisdom and understanding are more precious than gold and silver. Rhythms and cycles of creation were made when wisdom co-partnered with God at the beginning of time.

Prayer: Unseen realities of eternity are mine today – I acknowledge and agree with Your thoughts and perspectives, all-knowing and magnificent God! I want to know how to respond as You would, and to act accordingly.

God is saying to me:

_____

_____

_____

_____

_____

_____

The Royal Invitation

1. REPENT AND BE BAPTISED (turn away from sin. Sin is transgressing God's laws).

Mark 1:15, Jesus said, "Time's up! God's kingdom is here. Change your life and believe the Message." (MSG)

Acts 2:38, Peter said, "Change your life. Turn to God and be baptized, each of you, in the name of Jesus Christ, so your sins are forgiven. Receive the gift of the Holy Spirit. The promise is targeted to you and your children, but also to all who are far away—whomever, in fact, our Master God invites." (MSG)

He commands us all to repent and turn to God. (Acts 17:30b TPT)

2. BELIEVE (be confident in the reliability of God's Word).

1 Thessalonians 4:14 (TPT) – For if we believe that Jesus died and rose again, we also believe that God will bring with Jesus those who died while believing in him.

No one earns God's righteousness. It can only be transferred when we no longer rely on our own works but believe in the One who powerfully declares the ungodly to be righteous in His eyes. It is faith that transfers God's righteousness into your account! (Romans 4:5 TPT)

This how much God loved the world: He gave his Son, His one and only Son. And this why: so that no one need be destroyed; by believing in Him, anyone can have a whole and lasting life. (John 3:15 MSG)

3. CONFESS

...For if you publicly declare with your mouth that Jesus is Lord and believe in your heart that God raised him from the dead, you will experience salvation. (Romans 10:9b TPT)

This is the beginning of a lifelong journey of knowing God and knowing your place as a son/daughter in his family.

Protect this precious salvation gift by:

o   reading His Word

o   speaking to Him

o   learning to hear Him

o   sharing your faith, and

o   meeting regularly with like-minded believers

o   be water baptised and filled the Holy Spirit

ABOUT THE AUTHOR

Roz is a retired teacher who has a passion for God, family, people, the outdoors, and travel. She enjoys poetry, journaling and has exhibited and sold several paintings. She is a revelation interpreter who loves inspiring and encouraging others in the next phase of their walk with God.

Roz immigrated from South Africa to New Zealand in 2009, where she lives with her husband, Roy.

Roz & Roy have two adult daughters and a son-in-law.

If you have been encouraged by this book, Roz would love to hear from you. You can contact her at rozinnes.creative@gmail.com

CPSIA information can be obtained
at www.ICGtesting.com
Printed in the USA
BVHW021704140422
634330BV00019B/404